A MONS_ OF A CO_

Contents

The Strange, Strange World of Weird — 2
By Robin Etherington and Zak Simmonds-Hurn

Dinosaurs Around Us — 6

Crab Lane Crew — 8
By Jim Medway

The Strange, Strange World of Weird — 12
By Robin Etherington and Zak Simmonds-Hurn

Sausage and Carrots — 16
By Simone Lia

MEET THE AUTHORS

ZAK SIMMONDS-HURN
Creator of THE STRANGE, STRANGE WORLD OF WEIRD
LOVES: drinking tea, cartoons, fruit crumbles.
HATES: exercise, waking up early and cold tea.

ROBIN ETHERINGTON
Creator of THE STRANGE, STRANGE WORLD OF WEIRD
LOVES: snowboarding and toast... seriously, he can go through a whole loaf in five minutes!
HATES: early mornings, jacket potatoes and sunburn.

GRRRAAAA

"Ah... yes. Now I see."

"Can I call you back?"

"Run!"

"Run faster!"

"The only idea I can think of is..."

"RUN AWAY!"

"Quick, everyone get in my police car!"

"Lowe, that thing is heading straight for us. What are we going to do?"

"We'll save Teresa's doughnuts, you start the engine!"

DINOSAURS AROUND US

We all know that dinosaurs are **extinct**. The last dinosaurs died out 65 million years ago. But their closest relatives are still alive.

Many scientists think that there is a creature alive today which is related to the terrifying Tyrannosaurus Rex. Can you guess what it might be? You could be surprised, as it is ... the chicken!

Scientists looked at the **protein** inside dinosaur bones. They found the same protein inside chicken bones.

Other animals alive today look a lot like **prehistoric** creatures. Crocodiles haven't changed the way they look in 200 million years.

Lizards existed millions of years ago and they looked a lot like they do now. The largest lizard in the world is the Komodo Dragon. You can guess how it got its name! It can grow to over 3 metres long, and can knock animals over with a swing of its tail.

Extinct
All died out.

Prehistoric
A time before there were people writing about what was happening.

Protein
Something inside bodies that makes cells grow properly.

Sausage AND carrots

Simone Lia

Johanna Carrot and Stanley Sausage are playing a board game.

"I don't want to play any more."

"It's no fun playing with you. You always win – I want to be the best at something."

"I know what you're the best at."

"What?"

"Losing badly!"

"I knew I was good at something."

Joke: What's the best thing to do if a monster breaks down your front door? Run out the back door.

Riddle:
Q. How can you leave a room with two legs and return with six legs?
A. Bring back a chair with you.